A CALL

Celia E. B. Thompson

Sierra Leonean Writers Series

A Call

ISBN: 978-9988-8698-7-8

Sierra Leonean Writers Series

120 Kissy Road, Freetown, Sierra Leone
Kofi Annan Avenue, North Legon, Accra, Ghana
Publisher: Prof. Osman Sankoh (Mallam O.)
publisher@sl-writers-series.org
www.sl-writers-series.org

Dedication

With intense gratitude to King Jehovah, I dedicate my first book to the love of my life; my first child, Queen Adelia H.E. KOH, and my dearest mother, Francess Elizabeth Thompson. They were the first ones I would read my poems to and then wait for their invaluable critiques.

CONTENTS

Part One – Poems in English

Part Two - Poems in Krio

Acknowledgements

I recognise the motivational support I received from Mr. Abdul Tejan-Cole, Director of OSIWA and his lifetime introduction to Professor Osman Sankoh (Mallam O), SLWS publisher, who has worked with me tirelessly to make this collection see the light of day. It has been a tedious but worthy journey. I also acknowledge members of the Sierra Leone Writers Forum (whatsapp), for their critique which helped formed and added tremendous value to my work. *Una tenki tenki!*

Preface

After over a decade of peacekeeping mission experiences and observing different cultures and family systems, putting this collection together, was a way to unload my conscience and make, 'A Call'. What legacy is 'today' building for 'tomorrow'? is the underlining question repeatedly posed in the variety of themes and imageries, whether it is deceit, corruption, impunity, dishonour, migration on the dark side, or love, hope and rebirth on the sunny side. I do not have the answers to the questions but as I grope around this space called 'earth' and interact with 'the others' that I share it with, I observe how, 'us' humans, recklessly treat others, our environments and state institutions and then greedily 'collect' everything for 'I'. A second issue that fights for my attention with more unanswered questions is that of the 'in betweens' in the life of the 'migrant'. On one side of the coin, he/she leaves his family in an 'underdeveloped' and 'unjust' society to get the greener apple on the 'other side'. There, he will struggle to be integrated into a new society- adopting different cultures and ideologies. On the other side of the coin, he has his indigenous obligations- family and community- to keep up with. The nexus between the issues of his two different 'worlds' becomes shaky. A shakiness, that in most cases would eventually leave him in a confused state of 'return' or 'no return'; a gap which he must bridge to prevent a 'cut-off' between his two 'worlds', if he ever makes it to the 'otherside'.

Celia E.B. Thompson
Irag, 5th June 2017

PART ONE - POEMS IN ENGLISH

A Call

Yesterday, my mother called, not to schedule her return
But, to boast of her no return
Yesterday, my father called, not to console my grandma
But, to plan his no return

Yesterday, my grandma cried, not to regret her silent pang
But, for my dark tomorrow
Yesterday, the neighbours cried, not for my grandma
But, for 'our' empty tomorrow

This morning, she told me a different story, not to amuse me
But, to make a call
This morning, she died, not because she was sick
But, because she lost hope to call

Today, I will call my mother, not for her return
But, to make a call
Today, I will call my father, not to bury grandma
But, to make a call
A call for my tomorrow!

Hear me, O vulture!

It is food not pleasures which I yearn for
Hunger not lust which I parade for;
prematurely weaned, reaped from my suck
It was not I that uncovered my nakedness
So, cover me in your wings
but not to scoop my honour away

It is home not pleasures that I knock for
Protection not dishonour, which I pray for
I did not know that my nakedness
could ignite such cravings
Cover me in your wings
but not to tear my honour for spoils

It is love not pleasures which I thirst for
Hope that my tomorrow will be covered
You must have seen my nakedness from your height;
my wobbling feet balanced on bruised sole
When you spread your wings
do not wound my honour.

Don't steal my news

I was going to make good news
but you drugged and trafficked me; and
in my shame and dishonour
You made me the news, for you

I was going to break good news
then you raped me on the train; and
in my battered bloody state
You made me the news, for you

I was going to tell the news
then you shot me on my way to school; and
in my unconsciousness
You made me the news, for you

I was going to make news for my parents
then you kidnapped me, massacred my friends ; and
as our parents mourn us
You made us the news, for you

It must be that you lack the salt to make your own news
But if you were to make your own news
without me being trafficked,
raped, shot or captured
then I will be free and secure
to make news for myself

Life's luxury

Break a smile
erase the wrinkles
but even with a wrinkled smile
break smile as a luxury

Spill out stuffed laughter
challenge the reproach
but even with a shameful laughter
spill laughter as a luxury

Pick a dance
shake out the fear
but even with a fearful dance
pick dance as a luxury

Make peace
Distil your heart
but even with a stifled peace
make peace as a luxury

Rebirth Africa!

Tonight, I conspire with Orion and Mazzaroth
As Arcturus guides my husband.
Whitely adorned I lay in quiet tension
to perform my conjugal rights with a purpose.
Tonight, I receive strength from his loins
to conceive for a purpose
Tonight, pleasures are taboos; as
our ancestors revoke greed, injustice and immorality
I take my position to perform;
with one purpose I must conceive.
The clock ticks. The sun warms my face.
It is time.
My conspirators take their positions
Whitely adorned for this purpose
I lay in position to perform
The heavens witness this bloody purity as
skilled midwives guide my actions.
With a purpose our ancestors invoke oneness, justice and morality.
A bloody head thrust out breaking the tensed silence
with his deep cries.
This one arrives with a fist
He will be washed in the calabash; as
the fifty-four break kolanut but there will be no dancing but
only the drums with a matching beat, as
our ancestors bury the cord deep in the soil and depart.
I arise and wait.

Strangled Lion

An angina has gripped my heart
    brutally moving to clout my retina
seizing my vocals
    I cannot roar for the safety of my pride
If I die, another will take over and eat my cubs
    my pride destroyed
With such cruelty it attacks to paralyse me
    Will I die before the mocking eyes of my preys?
My pride taken over
    as my cubs become meals for another?
And me, a crownless King
    my carcass reproached.
But If I can fist before it clogs my aorta
    and congeals my corrupt blood,
I will roar for the safety of my pride
call this jungle to order
and restore my pride
With a moment's breath,
I will roar!
for the blood of Sengbe Pieh and Bai Bureh run in my veins.
I will roar!
for preys to tremble,
call the jungle to order, correct the wrongs
and restore my pride.
I must fight this angina to be able to redeem my pride!

When did it rot?

When did it rot?
Before Gbana's imprudent act of 1788
or after the Nova Scotian settlement in 1792?
Before Bai Bureh was whisked off to the Gold Coast
or after 'the Gunners' revolt?
For posterity, I ask.

When did it rot?
Before we flew the Jack Union
or after Milton Margai waved the 'Green, white and blue,' in 1961?
Before Siaka Stevens said, 'pass a day'
or after Joseph Momoh pleaded guilty?
When did it rot?
Before Foday Sankoh let hell loose in the 90s
or after the junta?
Before Leonardo said 'blood diamonds'
or after the 'Aljazeera logging episode'?
For posterity, I ask.

When did it rot?
Before it's children shook off the dust underneath their feet
or after they refused to return home
Before it was referred to as 'Athens of West Africa'
or after I wrote this poem?
For posterity, I ask.

Distil me not!

For bigger excreta
larger carcasses
ruptured foetus
toxic wastes
newer rats
distil me not!
For I will still emit
pungent smell like
the village abattoir
the Abortionist room
and still cover bigger rats
So, if not for lavenders or roses
if not for cedars or palm trees
distil me not!

White lie!

Thorn honour clothed in white
Stained honour veiled in white
Empty vows erected in white
Defiled symbols gloved in white
All applaud lie in white
Unveil me to show teeth in white
Performed when flashed white
Suppress blood for white
Moan for petals, whitely
Witnessing a lie in white
Satin in white
Blood turned white
No anxious parents in white
For they know the lie is white

I came to pray

I came to pray on this pedestal
for the pedestrians
on the left, right and the others going across.
Their destinations I know not
but if it be beyond the seas
I came to pray
that they will not shake off the soil from their feet
and their hearts will remain home

I came to pray on this pedestal
to the Celestial
for the drivers turning left, right and the others going across,
that at their stations they will work diligently
and their hearts will remain home

On this pedestal I came to pray
for the preys
for swift flight from their predators
and their safe return, home

I came to pray on this pedestal
for my pallies
that when next we meet
they will remember to pronounce my name correctly
and we will lick palm oil with our fingers from my mother's
kitchen.

Money showeth man

I see them, look at them;
come as preys
leave as scavengers
come as victims
leave as perpetrators
come spirit-filled
leave possessed
come in servitude
leave as slave masters
I see them, listen to them;
come in reticent
leave in arrogance
come as Adam
leave as Solomon
I see them, smell them;
come dirty, leave dirtier
come thirsty, leave thirstier
come hungry, leave hungrier
come angry, leave angrier
I see them, I know them;
come in empty, leave loaded
with an empty heart.

My Frenemy

I knew not that Iscariot spat in your mouth
So like Jesus, I let you kiss me
I knew not that the Serpent kissed you
So like Eve, I ate the apple
I, not being Davida, sent my husband to hell
and conceived on my neighbour's bed
the bastard is your god son

But now that I know who thou be
I shall open my eyes when you kiss me
watch the apple you offer me
and listen carefully to the counsel you give
For when next we meet
it will neither be at the garden
nor before the Roman Soldier

My nights!

Come, I'll tell you about my nights
One night can unfold in different colours; but the
grumbling clouds forewarn this night will be the 'standing one'
for the stars are not here.
There will be on mosquitoes but the wolves will come sniffing for
meat
They tear without mercy; their right, I guess.
Hunger!
Lightening accompany thunders and the motorists wash me
Their right, I guess.
Safety!
The waters caress my shaky legs but I am not alone
If the waters do not get my neck and I out swim the reptiles
you will not find me on the slab.
Oh! the siren chimes.
That is another night.
But if the morning sun greets me, I will tell you about a different
night
How is your night?

My mornings!

Hurry, my mornings are not for snails
The slab I escaped, so, I take to the street; fist for fist.
The wolves sniff from their corners; their rights, I guess.
Breakfast!
But where is mine?
Ouf! I'll have the half rotten oranges after sweeping the stalls
Some bad creditors I have here; their rights I guess
Profits!
The 'others' pay but they cannot put up with my smell
and they think I hail from the 'Ali Baba' clan
Can I say otherwise?
They can't hear me from the distance; and
if I insist, I will not escape the bars.
Will you come for me?

Not in my dream

If I were to script my dreams
You, will be a fly on the wall
and if you fuss
I will smash you
Because with you in my dreams
I cannot locate Orion's belt.
If I were to invoke emotions in my dreams
You, will be revoked
to escape bad luck and nightmares
If I were to edit my dreams
I will crop you and then
thrash you,
for you have lost your space in my dreams.

Odourless

When I first met you
I could smell you without seeing you
For I knew your smell
you smelled like breast-milk
and even when you started smelling
like vanilla strawberry
and then like lime
I could still smell you without touching you
The next time we met
you smelled like Chameleon;
you carried a sweet tingling burning scent
that provoked my nose
and it became difficult for me to smell you
I had to see or touch you, to know that it was you
Now, I cannot smell you at all; and
Even when you stand next to me
When I see or touch you
I cannot smell you
I must be losing my sense of smell
Or you,
your sweat glands?

Red, for the Nile girl

For you, I wear red
I threw my black on your box
You, priced at birth
sold after the first crack of the egg
ill-luck beauty reared for cows
mowed for a dowry.

For you, I will wear red
You, who came in black
plucked in green
left in black; not a word of your own.
You, with a sealed destiny,
how much story can you tell from your reddened eyes?

For you, I must wear red
You, reared for the cows
dumped after the cows
should have been dumb like your mother
locked-in like your grandma.
You, whose value is in the cow,
for you, I wear red!

The 1 Ghc pain

Blood shot eyes on strained neck,
clenched teeth suppress inner pain
underneath a silver-coloured pan.
Saddened eyes tell of a deeper pain
other than the load it carries in the pan.
A flashed laughter opens the heart of the eyes as
brows deepen folds to unfold panoramic images of
        disbelief
        rejection and
        subjection....
Resolution sharpens and another image of hope appears
to quickly disappear
underneath the silver-coloured pan
for 1 Ghc

Daddy is at the ENT

At the reception
I pray for restoration of daddy's hearing.
His ear drum must be preserved so
that he can hear the coming noise and protect us.
These days daddy does not hear anything

At the reception
I told the receptionist
about daddy's deteriorating sense of smell.
He must be able to smell the rot
and prevent the decay in the family.
These days daddy does not smell anything

At the reception
I cried for Daddy to regain his voice.
If the doctor restores his vocals,
daddy will once again
teach us to sing: ' I will exalt thee, realm of the three....'
These days daddy does not say anything
I am waiting for daddy at the ENT

Dangle me no more rules

No more rules for me
No google on the
'10 rules of how to love'
nor Youtube on the
' 10 rules on ethics of life'
You, not the internet, will be my role model
I will watch and learn from you
So, I will fail in your failure
and succeed in your success
I forbid any more rules
to corrupt my innocence
and widen the vacuum of my ignorance
Show me how to be respectful and I will show respect
Show me how to strive for excellence and I will excel
Show me how to be content and I will not be greedy
You, will become my example
and I, your indicator
For if you see me falling and failing
it will be because I am a product of
who you are and what you have made out of me

Happily married?

When are we happily married?
Is it when we act naturally
for our family?
Or when we are clearly misunderstood
in our neighbourhood?
If our loving
is found missing
and there is a conspicuous absence
of our kindness,
are we still happily married?
What if when we are alone together
our bodies are freshly frozen,
should we make a sweet parting
and cut off this sweet nonsense?
or should we just loosely tie
this knot for a definite possibility
of staying happily married?

I found a boyfriend

I found a boyfriend.
We shared popcorn over James Bond
and he did not touch my lacy panty when the lights went off.
I had a bad day and cried on his chest and
he did not lick my tears away or touched my breasts
He talked to me on how to be strong.
We went dancing and I got drunk and
he did not take me to his bed;
he took me home unruffled.
I found a boyfriend who
proudly walks with me around the neighbourhood
and watches out for me in the dark
He is unfriendly to his friends who want to tear me.
With my boyfriend, I can freely make mistakes
Yes! I found a boyfriend; a friend in a boy.

My two-toned boo

When he is my boo, he woos me,
beats honey to sweetness
and his tongue intoxicates me like sweet red wine.
He comes to my bed warm; wakes in a cuddle
tells the silliest jokes, brightens my dull ones
calms my storms and breaks a storm in my stomach
This boo will sting for me
and makes my predators his preys

When he is mama's boy, he boos me,
vinegar is sweeter and his teeth bites my tongue.
He beats the chameleon to camouflage;
huffs and puffs
and my food smells foul.
He comes to my bed cold and even the harmattan feels warmer
This mama's boy will sting me
side with my predators and makes me his prey
My boo is two-toned
Don't even know which colour he woke up in today.

Same Woman

Little tears you spilled in anger,
muscling weak strength in confrontation,
a defense against this devil.
Small folds around her neck
for haphazard protection, you offer
to protect her from this devil
You would face Goliath

Years later,
the little boy becomes his father
who would show no mercy;
spill no tears
offer no protection.
Yesterday, he cried for his mama
Today, he wrings the neck of his wife
Who can deliver this woman from this devil?
Who can face this Goliath?
For she is the same woman

The Mourners

At this funeral
only professional mourners will cry.
Upon my cue
they will cry according to rehearsals
For them, I know why they cry
and I know that I will still see them after the funeral.

Not you crying the loudest
sniffing were water fails
mumbling underneath your breath.
For you, I know not why you cry
and I know that
I might never see you after the funeral.

The professionals, not you
will be at the graveside
For them, I know why they play this scene;
not you, who feels the wood of the coffin,
and then takes a selfie.
Not you, who insist on blinking sleeping tears,
because you do not mourn.
At this funeral,
only professional mourners will cry.

The seed does not die

She plants a seed with the hope
for it to blossom and brightens her.
She waters and waits
and then waits and waters,
but the seed sprouts not.
In her eyes, the seed died
and her heart died because she did not see
the seed growing roots.
Every day she looks at the spot
and sees nothing.
Then one morning,
a little flower said, good morning.
The root was mature to blossom.
She now understands
that all she has to do is to
water and wait,
then wait and water,
for the seed to greet her.

Woman's woes

She was human
long before she became a woman;
then a woe, for a man.
Sometimes, she is an ashtray;
if she is not a dustbin, she is a toilet seat.
For her holder's pleasure, she is a dog;
can play many tricks which she learnt from the other dogs.
For his exercise,
she is a punching bag and then, a mat
which he can use in turns with his friends.
On a good day, she is a junkie;
achingly begging for an holler coaster trip
But on a sales day, she is only an item;
devoid of her soul and spirit,
packaged to be transported to hell.

A jewel in the garbage

Buried too soon
Birthed in darkness
Swaddled and thrown to be forgotten;
not chanced to shine.

Dumped to fall deeper,
layers of covers choke its breath;
your stomps bury even deeper.
Don't look too far for it's under your feet;
a 'jewel mine' buried in the garbage
to be forgotten.

Buried too deep,
this jewel might never make the classy show glass,
miss the soft touch of the jewellery's gloves;
no display.

But, if you look deeper, it will glitter at you.
If the muscles in your back would allow you a bend,
you will find a jewel deep in the garbage
Will you dig it out?

If you could bend down,
there are more shines deep in the soil
buried underneath your stomps,
mingled and bred in dirt;
it's worth unknown.

So, all call it, 'garbage'.
But, if your hand can touch that smelly soil,
you will find a jewel in the soil.

Let me hug you

Say something
and shut up this loud silence!
Only your eyes have been talking;
pictures too bizarre,
resolution too dull .
Where are you bleeding from?
Let me hug you I implore you,
I need to hold you
for that is all I can offer you now;
'trust' and 'love', I do not have to offer.
Those bitter bloody eyes;
eyelids shutting
on voluminous scary balls.
You should not be seen like this,
let me hug you and melt those glaciers.

Do something
and quiet this ominous bird.
Spit out the blood
and un-choke the clots.
Bloody teeth clamping
on dry smelly tongue
Let me hug you, for that's all I have.
Let me offer these harmless shoulders
for you to bleed your soul out on.
Before we engage in an 'Hammam ritual',
the goddess will chose the spices.
Another day,
we could try to redefine 'trust' and 'love'.
But for now, let me hug you.
No one should see you like this,
let me hug you and melt those glaciers

Mama is bleeding

Mama is bleeding;
a ripped vein leaking.
In good time, a surgery might
stop the haemorrhage.
The Lion is bleeding helplessly
She, who roared to birth them
as the thunders broke their silence behind the mountains,
cannot even fist.
She has been logged;
a ripped vein leaking

Mama, who brought home all the food
has become a defenseless prey
but, inedible,
only fit for reproach and mockery.
With over-sucked breast and
wrinkled stomach,
mama lay wasting;
reaped, ripped and leaking

Selflessly, she gave it all;
Bauxite, Iron Ore, Gold, Diamond, Rutile
and even more,
Limenite, Chronite and Platinum.
Even those who visited got something
No homage, no royalties!
Once 'Athens of West Africa' is bleeding
Who will stop the haemorrhage?

My brother's confession

"I lost my innocence long before you did," confided my brother.

"You were scorned and scorched, but me, society applauded my defilement. My voice broke; my boyhood botched, not a word as I dined with the devil on the same table as you did," he exposed.

"You lost your confidence; while I gained a dirty confidence underneath the blind watch of our parents. I grew taller, perfecting my dirty act, not a word," he admitted.

"Every time I saw your tear stained eyes, I inwardly cried with you but suppressed my revolt," explained my brother.

"You exhibited your tears and I, favoured society. I grew longer and tougher; filed in, not a word," moaned my brother.

"I think that I am as mad as you are with a desecrated mind," cried my brother.

'Except that when you ask for help, I fear to escape this labyrinth for the abyss, pin the cocoon and dissolve this Utopia," confessed my brother.

Mama's driving notes

Driving notes from my mother
are lesson notes for a mother.
The signs,
colours,
go, stop, slow down, make a bend,
one way, double way, no way, high way,
low beam, high beam,
emergency, reverse, turn around;
all notes for a mother

Yesterday, my mother shared her driving notes.
She has stopped at many red lights,
moved on when they turned green,
missed some of her turns,
went off route, and then,
came back to take the right ones;
but she has never stopped driving

She says the curves can be tricky
and the noise deafening
when the lights are not working.
She becomes tensed behind the wheel,
waiting for the opportunity to drive on,
watches out for the police
to avoid the ticket,
but, if found wanting, she takes one,
but, she has never stopped driving.

She uses the one way,
turns into the two way,
joins the high way,
drives on the left side,
signals to join the right side,
steps sharply on her brakes,

33

uses the emergency light,
makes sure that she stays on the road
to reach her destination,
she has made some few bangs,
fought with other drivers,
but, she is still driving.

My pink and blue, not faded

What you are dragging on are shades of pink and blue
not the pink and blue which I fly.
My Pink and Blue are not your shades of pink and blue;
bright and attracting, envy when it flies.
Your pink and blue are faded and dotted with stains,
still at half mast
Mine are the two that resonates with excellence;
symbols of strength and pride in each strand
Faithful to exhibit her virtues,
her prowess in producing excellence
from each strand.
That's how I became
a peacock with pink and blue feathers
and in these colours I soar like the eagle.
My unflinching love for my pink and blue
will not become daunted by your mistreatment
because, what you are dragging on are shades of pink and blue;
a mirage, not my brand.
My pink and blue are a distinction not on extinction
My pink and blue, will always be
'Esto fidelis'

Remember Her- Hannah (August 2015)

What do I do with you now
in your battered bloody body?
If your eyes were not glued
I could watch the last pictures you saw
and tell your story differently.
What a picture you were made; when captured
must be nominated for all the details it present
What did you see before they were shut?

What do I say to you now
in your drenched drugged deafness?
If your lips were not glued
I could have seen your last emotions
and write your story differently.
What a sight you were made; when looked upon
must be nominated for all the aspects it present
What were you saying before you were shut up?

Let me hug what was left of you
for that is all I can offer you now
Justice, I do not have to offer
a $1000 might never be paid
You are not the first
Let me hug you, for that's all I can offer
Justice, I cannot promise any

No one saw you dragged, gagged, raped and sealed
I could have taken you for an 'Hamman ritual'
but it would not clean your inside.
So, I will hug what was left of you,
cry with your mother,
lay a flower by your troubled blood,
light a candle for you;

And then,
Wait!

Remember Her; Haja Kamara (23yrs- May 2016) (sequel to Remember Hannah)

Hannah: Hush now, you have been crying day and night
Haja: I want to cry the more….(frightened) I saw him
Hannah: hush now….He cannot get you here
Haja: (still crying) you are still bleeding
Hannah: Yes…that's how I cry now
Haja: I saw him
Hannah: I saw you on our forum
Haja: After I was raked
Hannah: then you were disgraced
Haja: (still crying)
Hannah: they shared your naked pictures as if it was a leaked paper
Haja: (still crying) As if I am not their own….of the same soil
Hannah: (laughing)
Haja: I saw him!
Hannah: Mine?
Haja: Ours?
Hannah: The cameras! They must have seen him
Haja: (laughs through her sobs)
Hannah: The other girls!
Haja: I think he is going to get them
Hannah: (starts sobbing) He is going to get them
Haja: His preys are naked
Hannah: A $1000?
Haja: Maybe $2000 for me…no Madarin speaker where I come from?
Hannah: was that him?
Haja: (continue crying)……
Hannah: quiet confusion….whiles he enjoys his preys
Haja: When are you washing the blood off?

Hannah: Never!
Haja: (still crying) then let me cry.
And then;
we wait!

The body in blue shorts-January 6, 1999

I never forgot about you
I have seen you in my dreams a thousand times
I have spoken about you countless times
I, who only have words for you;
after your abrupt transition
on that hot afternoon on January 6
From across the Nursing training school, I cringed
when the men in green
brought you in their green van, and
threw you from a green stretcher
half naked, fair and pale
in your blue shorts
soaked in fresh blood, which I guessed was yours
My suffering mother stifled my vomit
scared that my grumbling stomach
was loud enough to draw attention
For I, was also a culprit; a student.
From my hiding place, I stole another glance at you
as my heart located your mother
seeing your blood embracing the soil
They briefly scanned the area and left,
there was more work to do.
I saw you,
The clouds will bear me witness.
When we meet next, please tell me it was you.
And I will tell you what happened after you closed your eyes

A selfie

Look at what my predilection
for selfies has on exhibition;
a face!
Crowned with weak
silver tinted hair, stripped with golden strands which lazily
falls on a wrinkled neck
to accentuate aristocratic attitude
a pale tired skin over-pampered with rich make-up
exhibit huge beautiful eyeballs infested with
cataracts neighbouring a dull iris.
A face,
on which hung a
Heavy-rimmed glasses carelessly perched
on a broken nose
I like the blood red lipstick attempting to
glow the thick cracked lips that cover
white-washed teeth
A strained smile which enlarges
withered ears
exposes a lost pair of canine
and broken incisors.
My office selfie is ugly!
Another take!

<u>Who am I?</u>

Let's rebel this time
one against the other
for sanity's sake.
At this height
I must exorcise my jailer
and transit my weakness;
unchecked.
Let me for once be my master
weak to exhibit my imperfections
strong to celebrate my perfections.
One against the other
let's separate;
unwaged
For there is no union in our unity
and me, a stranger in this trio
caged
clipped
to rage
Become an enemy even to my own shadow,
shoot it
when I need it to follow
for my adrenalin
shoots and hoot
juggling my senses
with no direction of mine.
I am a weakling;
engage my fists in talks
dumb in my talks
trapped
in my insecurities
A stranger I have become in this game
tossed

possessed
played by spirits
making their 'Captain call'
at my expense
The one empties me of humanity
and I display arrogance for weakness
while the other makes me a societal pun.
So, today I will do what
I left undone yesterday
rebel for sanity's sake
to find me
Who am I?

My small corner

My small corner is reserved;
a reservoir to distil
my lavatory
There, I go alone to wash
my intestines
my purgatory
My small corner is my dirty corner
for me, not you,
we do not smell the same.
There, I go alone;
brutally dirty
not for you to violate,
for there is only space for
'The Three'.
My Communion;
my small corner is
where I become empty and naked.
Expose my ugliness,
beat myself a thousand times
my purgatory.
My small corner cannot be invaded
It is where I take my bath,
fall to the bottom
and rise to see the top.
If I lose my small corner,
I will become a monster
not fit for 'The Three'.
If my small corner is invaded,
I will become corrupted
and destroy my bigger corner
I don't want you in my dirty small corner
It's reserved.

No blood for you

Before we solemnize this union,
I confess.
I did not come with the blood;
I lost it.
As a little girl, I prayed and vowed to do just that;
I failed.
The scene is flowery, but there will be no discovery;
Pedro was here.
I am sorry your morning will be filled with mourning,
I cry.
I broke the promise I made even to myself
I wanted you to arise and beat your chest with glitters in your eyes;
I failed.
My childhood mirror bears witness to my endless rehearsal
Hmmm!
The journey has been a long tiring one
and in my impatience I became greedy and foolish;
I ate it.
Without valour
I spilled it
Not that I inherited it, but I wanted to leave it as a legacy;
I killed it.
This was not supposed to be a night of confession
But who can imagine what stories your own body will tell?

Is papa home?

You've been lying in the shade for too long
waiting for mama to bring home the kill
hunting down even the hunters
to bring home the feed
You've been sprawled out for too long
lazily roaring to tell them that you are home
as we all wait for the return of mama
for she has more to do after delivery

Maybe it's time you and mama changed chores
Maybe it's time you went out and dared the world
Maybe it's time you stopped defending
Maybe it's time you stopped looking at us strangely
as if you were going to eat us
if Mama delays with the meal

Papa, if mama does not bring home the kill,
will you eat us?
If the jungle becomes tougher,
will you still be lying under the shade
and roar for the safety of the pride?
Or, will you just move on to another pride?

The angry stonechat

This Stonechat can throw all the stones
it can find
but it cannot be angrier than I am.
You can no longer perch on your favourite trees?
but so can't I
You can no longer build your nests?
but so can't I
You fly longer time to find a good shade?
but so do I
You lost your beloved village
with its scenery and serenity?
But so did I
You eat polluted fruits?
But so do I
You are losing your feathers?
But so am I
The ground is too wet for you to pick the soil?
But so it is
No one listens to you?
But so it is
No one thinks about you?
But so it is
You can no longer hear your own chirpings?
But so can't I
This bird cannot be angrier than I am
We are in this together.

The deserted Apiary

If we were all as busy
as we say we are
what a 'pollinated' world this would be
The skies will drip with honey
the fruits will be fuller
and the matrixes will be swollen

If the bees were still in their apiaries
and not flying around for who to sting
who would lack honey?

If we were all as very busy
as we say we are
what a 'proper' world this world be
The children will not die at birth
The guns will be buried, and
The world will not 'smell'

Well, maybe, we are busy
even busier,
but not doing what we say
we are doing
For we can only see the result
of what we are doing

The bee left unnoticed
maybe it realised it was being impersonated
For if the bees were here
Oh boy, what a 'pollinated' world this will be
but the apiary is deserted
the bees are not here

The fabric is torn!

Oath taken, oath broken
Commission in, commission out
Vow taken, vow broken
swear again;
di law na biskit!
Impunity sunbaths by the Cotton tree
Even you, reaped the fabric

Garbage in, garbage out
a cabbage of worms
Wishy-washy, dilly-dally,
rota-rata, boto-bata!
A 'garbage monster' programmed
adorned in a beautiful gown with a coloured hood
Even you, reaped the fabric

Syringe in, syringe out
Malaria? typhoid? who knows?
It could be Ebola! Another laboratory
ol day get sababu!
Even you, reaped the fabric

Gallon out, litre in
Measurement out, kilogramme in
Rotten ones for VAT, more taxes
aw fo du, na di system
Even you, reaped the fabric

Corruption in, anti out
Anti in, corruption out
just another oxymoron
tifi tifi, jankoliki

47

Even you, reaped the fabric

Mission in, mission out
Dollar out, dollar in
money miss road
Mediocrity programmed
to pontificate borrowed ideals
Even you, reaped the fabric

Visa in, visa out
Lottery in, lottery out
Walk the dessert, drown the seas
hide in alleys, wash the toilets
come back and litter the streets with water bottles
d nigger is back, 'ehneh?'
Even you, reaped the fabric

Scoop out, story leaked
brown envelop out, story skewed
story dies, truth buried
wans na God de sheb
even you, reaped the fabric

And now, the fabric is torn!

The girl next door admires me

She scares me;
girl next door
Eyes so big like the moon,
she gives me shivers
She wants to posses me
girl next door
with eyes so dark as an eclipse
shadows me
she wants to be me
She has been watching me
to replace me
Her eyes have been sending me signals
Every time we meet and lock in gaze
she says, 'I am you'
Her eyes like my hair, my dress,
my shoes and my handbag
As my shadow, she follows me
Her smiles so greedy has the power to
drain my blood
I cannot utter a word
How do I tell her, I am not me!
The hair is not mine and neither is the dress
and although I own the shoes and the bag
I want to ask her
if she has the spine to bag
what makes her wag
She is desperate to be me
The girl next door admires me
I am scared for her!

The same dancers

Another day;
same dancers of yesterday
burst out as genies
in their same drunk-sweaty gears
Their red tired eyes already intoxicated
Suddenly, as if hypnotized they get into another frenzy dance;
a fusion of different moves
well performed by the little dancers
The rhythm changes and the dancers fire-up
into another possessed dance
They are no longer in control,
only their bodies respond to the spirits of the drums
The female dancers moving their beaded waist skimpily covered in
raffia, luring the beast
A beast jumps up within the crowd
as if to exorcise the dancers to respond to a new note
Just as they begin to change their moves,
a different beast jumps higher
and repossess them
The dance continues;
one step forward, two backwards and back into the ring
Transfixed, my body begins to shake
but suddenly stops
What is the reason for this dance?
Which festival is this?

Twisted laughter

A transition wronged;
the rite was botched
depriving you of a safe arrival
You departed with brilliance and illumination
but never arrived your destination
You, so innocent and promising
has been botched
Something went wrong during your transition
switching the lights off your eyes.
Was it lack of strength, spirit or
was it lack of salt?
When did that brilliant fire in your eyes switched lights
to a strange light which redirected your paths to
where?
This light which only you see, has casts darkness
depriving all of a celebration
Why the sudden strange laughter?
This new laughter that only you know
brings so much sadness
The rite was botched;
   pilgrim aborted
   chronicle distorted
   destiny destroyed
Something happened during your transition
Not sure even you know.

Fake reality

Tonight, I was going to love you with madness
and passion
then the flashes came rushing
and stripped me off
leaving me pale and numbed
Forsake these lips that tremble under your kisses
they are not mine
For mine can no longer taste lies
I disown these wild fingers
that refuse to be tamed
and obey me
The hands navigating you through my contours
are mutinous
Believe not these lecherous eyes
that begs you
Mine knows 'The Lecher"
My shameless tongue you should avoid
for they are only playing your game
This heart that endures your love
is not mine either
For mine is frozen,
too cold for madness and passion
So, turn away from these breasts that
tantalize you with swollen nipples
If they were mine, they will loosen to your
deceitful fingers
Let's turn the lights on
for my lights went off

Not Tonight!

With artistically stained hands
I caress you as you bathe me in coconut oil
We drift in delusion, influenced
by the strong smell of sandalwood spiced with
Egyptian musk
We are united in this sweet sin that we have created
and together we should face the charge
Today, do not snatch honey from my mouth
For my itchy tongue I have not been greedy with
neither withheld my lips
With feral fingers I freely guide your weak hands
from contours to contours
leading you to the dark treasures holding
the secrets
So, with my beads in your hands,
why do you suddenly rush ahead of me
when you meet
the secrets?
Wait for me my love
Tonight, let's uncover the secrets together and enjoy
each and every surprises together
As I meet you stroke for stroke
heart beat for heart beat
let tonight be different
to experience the pleasures
When we glide with the increasing altitudes
I dont want to be here waving at you
Take me with you!

Is thy member bereaved?

O member!
art thou bereaved
to fall thy head between the mountains?
O member!
where is thy swollen smile
in return for your fellow's
feverish excited greetings?
Why art thou so cold
in the middle of the furnace?
When thou knockest
My matrix jumped
and signaled my vulva to give
passage
But no sooner you were enclaved,
you dropped.
O thou wicked and ignorant member
that knoweth not the needs of the vulva;
such, which it must be delivered from
O! thou deaf member who heareth
not the groans
nor countest the moans
Thou shalt not leave my chamber
Until thy learn to count a score
Thou shalt be vulva-cuffed
Until thou liftest thy head
and fulfil my matrx demands
For what is thy purpose
of coming here
if un-businesslike?
Why waste so much juice
on a withered member
Still mourning?

Looking...

I am looking
for a culture to learn and keep,
one to believe in and practice
A society to observe and obey,
one to embrace and live in
rules to guide me
and rest equally on all
I am coughing and spluttering,
dithering and slithering
as I grope
for a culture to share and teach
A society to build us,
rules and guidelines to make us better
I am searching and yearning,
craving and wailing
for a culture to pass on
A society to furnish
an identity to flag around
I am looking and revving,
dreaming and waving,
calling for a culture, not to torture
A society,
not to count a booty,
notoriety for the loots
One that have the rules and guidelines
to straighten the lines
I am looking for a culture
to keep and give

<u>The chequered Hen</u>

If she has lost some of her strongest feathers,
it's because she has to jump the fire and
fearlessly give them to the hawk
If she has lost some of her most colourful feathers,
it's because she has to dig to lay her eggs
and then keep them from preys
If her feathers are looking so ruffled,
it's because she has been all over the neighbourhood
teaching her cheeks the survival tricks
If her beak is so dirty,
it's because she has been breaking ground
to feed her cheeks
The hot water she knows awaits her
but she passes by the fireside
if her cheeks have wandered there

Though she might have lost some feathers here and there,
crows with an annoying crack;
she neither stops crowing
nor stops digging for her eggs
She neither stops covering them
nor shaking off the preys
She neither fears the fire
nor stops to beak for her chicks
She hears everyday that she will soon die,
she has seen her fellows die in the same place
but she wakes up every morning and crows,
whether in cage or free
she shakes of the dust
rearranges her remaining feathers
and starts her days chores
to and fro

So, before you only 'eat' the next
tell her she is the strongest
for she thinks she is the weakest
They told her so
They made her so
She believes so
What they did not tell her
was that she is a source of strength,
the roots that supports the tree
Tell her she is at her best
when she thinks she is at her least,
for it was when she lay
that she got swollen
and like the hen that she is, started to lay
what was gotten

My Artist

An unfinished article I remain;
roughly written in shaky letters
The power to uncover my nakedness
lies only in your hands,
yet you cover me with your hands
The right to reap off my suckling child
from her suck lies only in your hands
Yet, you help her suck without choking
Twice, did I transit from the labour room,
twice you counted me in Time
Only you know that I do
not smell like 'Jadore' or ' Poison',
yet you embrace me in such filth
to warm up my chilled dead bones
In my iniquities, I found only you
Countless times have I run away from you
and come back begging, yet as a husband
blinded by love, you wrap your hands around me
and cover me with big embraces
Only you know the talking of my heart,
those thoughts that even scares me
Yet, you listen to me when I call you
So, I come to say,
You are the only artist
with the right brush and paint
that can rework
this outlined sketch and make me
a finished polished piece.

The unfaithful wife

The door was wide open
so I came in
Not that I expected you to be busy
for you, are the faithful one
It is I,
who have always been the runaway
looking for what I still search for
I ran after strength;
came back broken,
bruised and shackled
I, who have exposed my nakedness
within and without,
have come back
skinless,
covered in shame
I, the prodigal wife,
who cannot be faithful to you
for my raven cravings
If I didn't know you well,
I would think that you will reject me
put me in the pillory
and expose my sins
If I didn't know you too well,
I would think you would
give me a divorce
and find another
But no, the door was open;
expectant
So I came in as I am;
used and abused
nothing to show for it
I, the selfish wife
gloating over material things

that I always loose
I have come back
as filthy as I am
begging for your mercy.

The dog and its bone

The dog and its bone;
who can separate the two
when even the life of the giver is endangered?
With watery eyes it salivates and wags
and then jumps to snatch
It plays the giver's game until
it gets the bone between his teeth
Now, a master of the bone, it forgets the giver and
as a hyena, it breaks and tears
like a vampire, he sucks and sucks

And then;

once the master is satisfied
and the bone is juiceless
it gives a large belch of satisfaction
and breaks wind.
It separates itself from its spoil
and as he strolls around lazily looking for another,
he scorns it from a distance
leaving it to dry in the sun

And then;

on a hot hungry day
he remembers and then
master dog with its tail between its legs,
returns to its vomit

Tick tock resolution

Tick -tock, tock-tick,
no slower, no faster
Yesterday is today;
a change perceived
a farce conceived
to be performed
Tick- tock, tock-tick,
wishes could be horses
when tomorrow becomes today
But when tomorrow
becomes today
and the tick, tocks
what happens to you?

Some wait by their beds,
others drift in a bottle
Some by the cross, on the mat
others on the bridge of life
The pastors and imams try to get it right
while congregation play along
A countdown ticks-tocks;
spirits converge, locks body
subdued for a timing
Resolution change
with every tick- tock, tock-tick,
a change balanced
a farce maintained.

Tomorrow

Tell me what you see in tomorrow
where all the superheroes play power
engulfing space for superiority
With so much tension,
who could stop Big Bang 2
where 'invented' could become 'inventors'
and gods could serve their subjects?

What do you see in a tomorrow
where all the 'greedlers' lead
amassing wealth for longitivity?
With so much tension
who could stop World War 3
where giants will gobble migets
and gods will salute a God?

Any thoughts about your tomorrow
where you put no legacies
but garner all for worms?
With so much tension
who can stop the Armageddon
when all have become pale and meaningless?

Tomorrow for the poor;
fair would be foul and foul, fair
Shakespeare's three witches
will still be flying on their broomsticks

Love for tomorrow
will be acted in the Latin America garden.
With so much sweetness
veneered with bitterness,
who can stop Adam and Eve
from birthing Cain and Abel?

Are you as worried as I am for tomorrow?
Tomorrow could be fun
Tomorrow could be run

Wake up now

Wake up now
there is more sleeping tomorrow
  the birds have chirped away
  the cocks have finished crowing
  the moon has changed shifts
So, wake up now;
there is more sleeping tomorrow

Stand up now
there is more laying down tomorrow
  the flowers have opened up
  the trees are waving
  the birds are building their nest
So, stand up now;
there is more laying down tomorrow

Speak up now
there is more silence tomorrow
  the rivers are busting their banks
  the glaciers are melting to swell the waters
So, speak up now;
there is more silence tomorrow

Move on now
there is more stillness tomorrow
  the battle grounds have moved
  the times are moving
  the frontiers blazing
So, move on now;
there is more stillness tomorrow

Where I come from

Where I come from
the sun is shining but the day is dull;
Cocks crow cracking
Birds chirp chirp as Dogs bark bark
Lions laugh as Hyenas dig
Fishes die in water
Flowers sleep too soon

Where I come from
the moon is shining, but the fireside is cold;
genius, if born, is killed
saviour, if seen, is crucified
fathers are shacklers as mothers are hustlers
dreamers dream dream
thieves are swaggers as rouges are champions
labourers are trotters
with only connection in heaven
and baboons die early

Where I come from
the rain is heavy, but the ground is dry;
childhood is rough hood as adolescence is falsehood
adulthood is pain hood as old age is childhood
legacies are stillborn
sex has ex, so, foetus is hanging in the balance
to live or to leave

Where I come from,
the mountains are beautiful but the climbers show despair;
education is in retention as protection is in detention
wealth is health as takers are makers
politics is sticky as crime is perfect
resources are sourced

justice is rusty as money is talky
fair is foul and foul is fair

Where I come from
my compatriots are asking questions
the children; who, after the placenta tears,
hears their mothers travailing
the youths; who, searching for their worth
know that the noose is loose
the adults; who, horrified at their cracked hands
stare at the trampled eggs
the old; who, imprisoned by despair
cry for the cloud to swallow them

Where do you come from?

My cancer is self deceit

So drenched and drowned in my own deceit,
double masked in this charade
So soaked and soiled in my own deceit,
a statue on the wrong lane
A wind to uncover me,
a bang to fall me
might be all I need for redirection
to change the dance to this ominous music,
remove the pinching shoe and
gracefully dismount the stages

So righteously right in my self deceit,
clocked in cassock of piousness
so hunched and hungry in my hubris skin
Blind as bat, my days and nights fused
A prick to deflate me,
a confession to break me
might be all I need for clarity,
to stop cheating my feelings,
unmask my heart and
divorce my fake soul.

Then, I will stand opposite you
run to the North, face the South, and then;
separate my East from my West
Demystify my inner to face you squarely;
unburden the cassock,
confess my fears,
handover the borrowed life,
pay the interests
and die my own death

My Christmas

I love Christmas; only Christmas
I love the mass for the mashed
The cool harmattan breeze ushers the Carols
as the trees dress white
and the sweet rain smells right
I love Christmas;
plenty to eat, plenty to give,
not a penny from me, not a penny for me,
but my siblings and I have plenty to nib, tear and eat.
We don't do the chase at Christmas;
our house is loaded with goads,
I choose what gifts I will pick up

I love Christmas; for
night singers share their takings
Too much to drink and eat
and more on boxing day, full course mixed up
At Christmas,
even if the mass forget to bring me clothes and shoes,
they are never greedy with their food
All of theirs, the visitors and even the dogs
I love Christmas
It comes once a year!

Not afraid of Ebola

Not afraid of Ebola
yet afraid of not knowing its source
while you reshuffle the resource
to fight its force
and expel the myths

Not afraid of Ebola
yet I fear you, you and you
with shudder if you extend a hand
open for an embrace
and sweat next to me
with your bloody eyes
Afraid to make the call
for the ambulance
and get the chlorine

Not afraid of Ebola
yet, I fear the lack of sensitization
preventing sanitization
Fear for our health workers
fully clad in a centre over-worked
Fear for my brothers and sisters
becoming grave sitters
fully covered
to get 'them' covered

Ebola! No!
yet, I fear what you do to me
if you steal the Ebola money
if you do not build the Ebola centres

if you count the Ebola profits over me
if you deprive me of proper Ebola information
if you quarantine me without service guaranteed
then, I fear Ebola

I fear Ebola
will reappear
with its bloody, shameful history
to make more;
diggers
orphans
widows
Illiterates
child mothers
loose structures
leave flowers and candles everywhere; and then,
scare all away

The anger of the single mother

She is angry for you, not at you
Now that it was done, what is to be done?
Her fate; no one to undo
So, she wants to fight to prevent a repeat
She is angry to correct a wrong
Angry at injustices with impunity
She is angry that it was her fault
So, she wants to heal her wound
She is angry for you not to be wounded
Eyes as sharp as a knife,
angry to fight for you that which fought her

She is fighting for you, not against you
But she will fight you, to fight that which fought her
She is afraid for you, not of you
The fears you see in her eyes are your fears
Try to read them well and get an understanding
The anger of the single mother is for you, not at you
Too bad that sometimes in her anger,
she slips into hunger
and she might loose the fight

The toddlers pure love

The toddler is my only best friend
the only one I freely toddle with
Pure love with the sweetest milky kisses;
whether black, blonde or brunette,
lame, strong or weak,
poor, rich or disfavoured
violated, rejected or unloved,
the toddler is my only true friend
Tethered to my heart,
teetering my emotions
The most innocent sweet milky smiles;
uncorrupted as undiluted
Pure eyes that only seeks love and laughter;
they touch softly, smile deeply
Fair is fair; no fouls
Love is love; no tints
Fear is fear; no acts
A cry is a cry; a genuine need
Anger is anger; a bond has been breached
The toddler is my only true friend and lover
Blind or sighted,
clean or smelly,
genius or dump,
The toddler is my best friend
We play the best games with fair rules;
a tickle for a tickle
a smile for a smile
The free sweet love from the toddler
makes me humbler;
the toddler is my only true love

Who to tell?

Everyone looks at me
yet, no one sees me
Everyone talks to me
yet, no one talks to me
I am blossoming in front of them;
plucked in their eyes
Yet, no one sees it
No one talks about it

At breakfast table
he gives his goodbye kisses
one on her mouth
another on my forehead
as my body coils and recoils
to the signals
These are the women
in whom he is well pleased
his pleasures for living

Mum is mum
Sisters are shattered
Brothers are disoriented
Neighbours are hood-winked
Spiritual fathers are hypnotized
Father is dead
I am numb

After dinner
the sweet cuddles begin
the night is very promising
and in this house
everyone dies at night
No wonder,

no one sees
no one hears
no one talks
So, who to tell?

I feel like...

I feel like a crowned Queen;
like I have ruled a kingdom before,
some land, where the people did not annoy the earth
and the harvesters were orderly and generous
I ruled in peace
I feel like a crowned chief;
like I have upheld the customs and traditions
of a land before
Some community, where the groups did not defile the earth
and the harvests were full and ripe
I presided justly
I feel like a respected mother;
some home, where the members lived woe less
and the siblings were selfless
I cared lovingly
I lived virtuously
Yet, my spirit tells me, 'It is not here!'
So I ask, 'Where have you been wandering?'

I feel like a bright star;
like I shone before
Some skies, where each star took its right position
I shone in splendor and might
I feel like I have lived there before;
where we cooked in the afternoons,
danced under the moonlight
as our would -be suitors singled us out
and then paid the dowry
Our wrappers were tighter and finer
Our feet smarter and swifter
Yet, my spirit tells me, 'It is not here!'

And this place, where we are right now, only my body knows
And my spirit will not tell my soul where it wandered

I feel like I have been loved before;
in some selfless heart, that knows no hate
There, I loved freely
and slept sweetly
Somewhere, somehow,
I feel it in my blood
It is in my head
My emotions
Music from outer cultures conjure memories
I see pictures that do not belong here
Where is this place that my soul has been before?

And then,

I feel empty;
nothing is deep
everything is rigged
I feel like I do not belong here
Yet, my spirit continues to haunt me of what it knows
Even you,
I feel like I know you, somewhere,
but not here
For everything here is strange
You were not the same, there
So, why don't we go back?
where my spirit knows
Not here!

<u>Decisions</u>

Decisions;
She makes them for progression
when she wants to forsake depression,
because she knows repression
will put her in detention
But,
she makes them not when in despair,
nor take them when happy
None she makes when the cloud is crying,
nor takes them when the sun is smiling
For who takes them when gliding the skies
only to reach earth and see Mount Everest staring

Decisions;
He makes them for progression
when he must forsake suppression,
decause he knows deterioration
will put him in extinction
But,
he makes them not when he is tall,
nor makes them when he is short
None he makes when the sun is in his face
and he won't be making any when in silhouette
For who makes them in a pot belly
only to be deflated and scorned by kwashiorkor

Decisions;
Can they make themselves?
Can they force their captors to make them?
What happens if they are not made?

Decisions;
I have made some tricky -creaky ones
and I might have to make some tacky -cranky ones,
as I laugh at some of the weaky-leaky ones that have been made for
me and cry at some of the nasty-rusty ones thrown at me
But,
I have seen givers make leaky-sweepy ones,
only for their takers to make snaky-bitty ones,
to leave their future in derision,
because of a decision

Decisions;
maybe, they are to be made only when the soul agrees with the
spirit.

Is it the 'eye' that corrupts the 'I'?

Is it the "eye" that corrupts the 'I'?
I thought the balls were guilty,
then I think about corruption
even when the balls are without light
and I see the 'I' battling with the 'eye'
'I'
Sweetly selfish,
constantly capricious,
leading the balls to indulge

Is it the 'eye' that leads the 'I'?
I thought the balls were vicious,
then I think about politics
even when the balls are covered
and I see the 'I' battling with the 'eye'
'I'
Plainly covetous,
quietly domineering,
truly dishonest,
leading the balls to convulse

Is it the 'eye that implicates the 'I"
I thought the balls were infected,
then I thought about greed
I thought about virtues
and I see the 'I' battling with the 'eye'
'I'
Vertically horizontal,
innocently corrupt,
virtuously stained,
leading the balls to indulge

Is it the 'eye' that kills the 'I'
I thought the balls were weak
then I thought about death
and I see the 'I' battling with the 'eye'
'I'
Strictly coward,
proudly begging,
certainly unsure,
leading the balls to indulge

The women are naked!

The women are naked;
heads shaved when they bowed to till
Sun scorching their skulls,
sweating blood on their journey to look for their honour
The women are naked;
Topless,
ripped off while they suckled their young,
breasts leaking
blood oozing
on their journey to find their strength

The women are naked;
wrappers ripped
kaleidoscope of colours
threads in disarray
wind blowing
on their journey to find equality
The women are naked;
shoes stolen
feet wobbling
On their journey to find their destination

The women are naked;
raped on the beach
Shared on whatsapp
uploaded on facebook
Silhouette on instagram
Masked on twitter
Hanging to virtuality
Roping equality
On their journey to find their identity.

The work in our walk

Will our work do the walk?
How far do we have to work this walk?
I am scared because I feel giddish
not because I am priggish
but because I wish
we can work the strength
to be vertical in our walk

We have been walking before 57
So, we should have some work
To post on some rock
But if our education is in a dock;
making us a mock,
when our beauty was in her punk,
then, where is the work in our walk?

We have been crying since the 60s
So if Nkrumah started the walk
When Selasie was on the throne
and the AU said its doing the work,
why do we have 54 in the dock
crying for the
Diops and Sankaras
Toures and Madibas
Selassies and Garangs,
when Nyerere showed us the walk to our walk

I am squeamish
Because our economy is childish
For we thought we heard integration
When they actually said disintegration
Drowning is the new swimming
and the fishes are thinking

If there is a change in living
If I cannot move in my own house,
nor speak the language of my cousin,
where is the work in our walk?

Our children are staring
because we are daring
with no caring
So when they are walking,
they are staggering
When they are talking,
they are stammering
When they are dancing,
they are jittering
And when they are looking,
they are crying
for the work in our walk

A Smile

What is in a smile;
a lean one
a broad one
a strong one
or a weak one?
Just a smile
Whether facial or hearty;
how could one gesture hold so much power,
to break
to melt
to annoy
or to please?

A smile is what;
the lips
the eyes
the face
or the teeth?
Just a smile
Whether crooked,
straight,
tight or light,
how could one action cause such a variety of reaction;
to smile back
to hold back
to look at
or to read from?

What says a smile;
the angle
the width
the depth
or the colour?
How could one gesture hold so much power;

to kill
to heal
to return
or to reject?

My hus-band

My hus-band,
this bond has become a band
You must have mistook our vow
for a row
our bond
for a band
Is it the ring?
If I give you back the ring
Will you bring back the bond
and become my husband
just the way you were
before you became husky?

My hus-band,
your tongue has become a thorn
You must have mistook our vow
for a down
my yes
for a mess
Is it the veil?
If I give you back the ring
will you bring back the bond
and become my husband
just the way you were
before you became husky?

My hus-band,
when did your hand lose their healing power
to became a weapon?
Yesterday, we stood on an alter
Today, we are in a ring
I must have bequeath you
with so much power
to hurt me

I must have been looking at the gown
when you were down
Let me take it off

Yesterday, we made a bond
when we took the band
The two of us,
our voices repeating the vows
Today, it becomes a band
beating our heart
shackled with a symbol that we must unshackle
When did I give you so much right to band me
and encircle me in a ring?
My hands no longer fit in the gaps of yours

My soul is choking my spirit
and my senses have become dull
Is it you,
or is it me?
My hus-band

A woman for every man

There is a woman for every man;
a man for every woman,
so why the criss-cross or the cross-criss
A woman who can offer the sacrifice
when the shrine is presented
The one that can light the fire
when the wood is provided
A man who can be presented for a sacrifice,
so why the dilly-dally or the dally-dilly
A man who can titivate her
A woman who can titillate him

There is a jewellery for every girl
A tuxedo for every man
So why all the upside down and down side up
A soul provider that touches the sole;
a woman for every man,
a man for every women
If he can find her,
she will see him
Her eyes will lead him in the dark
His hands strong to protect and shield her
So why all the loving lies
When there is one for everyone

See you tomorrow

See you tomorrow
But, when is tomorrow,
where is tomorrow?
Tomorrow; here, yonder
When is tomorrow?
Where is, here and
where is, there?
Is tomorrow
the next day
the next time
Here?
Yonder?
When is tomorrow?

Is there only a Today?
Now is now,
Tomorrow is when?
The next cloud;
when the sun rises or sets?
When is tomorrow?

What do we do in tomorrow?
Where do we meet?
How do I know it is you?
Would you recognize me?
Would the trees be the same?
When is tomorrow?
Where is tomorrow?
Is there only a Today?

When we say, 'See you tomorrow'
What do we mean?
Who promises you tomorrow?

PART TWO- POEMS IN KRIO

Natay fray fish ɛn `Gɔd to man`; wi yon

A want kasada bred ɛn natay fray fish
Nɔ gi mi kasada bred ɛn ɔyl,
na wetin dat?
Ya na watalo jɔngshɔn,
usay a kin bay krak kasade bred wit fayn natay
Dɛn mami nɔ tich unu?
A de go Limba kɔna fɔ go drink `Gɔd to man`
A kin ɛnjɔy am na di bambu kɔp;
a nɔ want wata pan am o
a nɔ want yist pan am
jes frɔm Gɔd to man
Natin fɔ Tɔmsin
Na kasada bred ɛn ɔyl grevi ɔlman de sɛl
A mit di Pa dɔn miks am wit wata na di buli,
ɛn nɔnbɔdi nɔ kɔmplen
bɔt mi go kɔmplen
A want mi kasada bred ɛn natay grevi
fo blɔf dɛn tɔrist wit wi yon
a want mi drai `God to man` na bambu kɔp
fɔ blɔf dɛn tɔrist wit wi yon

A nɔ wan chenj wi yon;
a jɛs wan mek am fayn
ɛn blɔf wit wi yon
kasada bred ɛn `God to man`

Nɔ kam pwɛl ya o!

Nɔ kam pwɛl ya o!
yu mit ya dɔn mek
' usai dɛn tay kaw, na de i de yit'
Nɔ kam pwɛl ya!
Lɛf wi nɔ,
na yu papa gɛt am?
Na wi yon biznɛz wi de pan
pul yu yay pan wi chap
Na ya wi pɔt de bwɛl,
nor kam pwɛl ya!
Di big wan dɛm de pan dɛn yon
wi sɛf de du wi yon na ya
wi nɔ ambɔg nɔbɔdi
gi wi wi kola ɛn du wetin yu want
Nɔ kam pwɛl ya o!
Noto wi bigin am o,
na so wi mit ya
we wi chap, di pa sɛf de gɛt
so duya nɔ kam pwɛl ya!
Nɔto wi pwɛl am o
na smɔl tin nɔmɔ wi kin tek
aw fɔ du?
nɔ yagba, yu go lan
na ya wi de sɔvayv o
Nɔ kam pwɛl ya!

Wetin dɛn sabi?

Wetin dɛn sabi?;
a nɔ no.
Dɛn papa nɔ kin de na os
dɛn mama kin go tray fɔ lɛ pɔt bwɛl
dɛn neba kin de wach fɔ laf
Wetin dɛn sabi?

Sontɛm de, papa kin kam tɛm fɔ slip,
mama kin de bay fɔl na pala
Nɔnbodi nɔ no we junyɔ bigin tif
na neba si we mɔmi jomp winda
den bigin laf
Wetin dɛn sabi?

Papa kin lay pan mama
mama sef de lay pan papa
Na so dɛn bigin lay;
dɛn fil se na so fɔ tɔk
den gladi se den don sabi tok
Mɔmi nɔ go skul o
i de wɛr di yunifɔm go lidɔm na ticha bed
ɛn bay pamflɛkt we ticha de sɛl
Wetin dɛn sabi?

Junyɔ bin de we papa de bit mama
i yɛri we dɛn neba de kos badbad kos
in sɛf go fɛt na skul ɛn chuk
i de rɔn trɔbul
Mɔmi nɔ pas BECE
bɔt di Pa ɛp am fɛn wok
i de go ɛn kam, de pas de skek wes
i lan fast aw fɔ ton lɛft to rayt

10 to 100, en los den fayl dem
Wetin dɛn sabi?

We pikin go ton mami ɛn dadi
wetin dɛn go tich dɛn yon pikin?
If dɛn ton lida
wetin dɛn go du fɔ dɛn pipul
Wetin dɛn sabi?

A nɔ de mɛn dɔg fɔ gɔvmɛnt

A nɔ de mɛn dɔg fɔ gɔvmɛnt
mi na bebi shaynshayn
we a tif Pita, a de pe Paul
afta ɔl
nɔto mi bɔn bɔbɔ
we a go sɔri fɔ am

Nɔto mi de kam mɛn dɔg fɔ in ona
if yu krach mi bak
misɛf go krach yu bak
fifti fifti
afta ɔl
rɔtin bɔdi blant Jizɔs

Na yaso, wi ɔl na met
so nɔto mi de kam wes pawda pan kondo
we Jɔn pamayn trowe na Jɔn rɛs
na Jɔn in sɛf go yit am
afta ɔl
tif tif, Gɔd laf

<u>Chiyaman fɔ layf!</u>

Yɛs bra, yu bɔbɔ de ya so
Na mi gɛda dɛn bɔbɔ fɔ lɛ wi mek di rod
Bra, na fɔ lɛf smɔl tin fɔ wi kol wata ɛn kugri o
usɛf no se di tin tayt bra, ɛn wok nɔ de
Nɔ wɔri bra a go was di motoka
mi na yu yon layv bɔbɔ

Chiyaman, dis ivintɛm we a kɔmɔt
wach Champyons lig a go kam fɛn yu ɛn di mami
A no se di mami mɔs pas mi besin
Pa, mi na unu yon bɔbɔ o
na in mek a nɔ de tek fulish fɔ una
if pɔsin mistek, a go damej am,
a swɛ bra

Chiya, nɔ fɔgɛt mi o, fɔ ɛni lili rɔban
yu no se dɛn bin sak mi
pan da ɔda wan we yu fɛn fɔ mi
Na mi padi dɛm go tif de o
ɛn gi wi ɔl bad nem
Bra, yu no se mi nɔ gɛt prɔblɛm
mi na usai mi tu de kɔt fo nɔmɔ a de fɛn
mi na u layv bɔbɔ.

Celia E. B. Thompson

Aw fo du, na di sistɛm

Hmm, aw fɔ du naw?
Wɛl, ɛnti na yu want yu biznɛs fɔ du
na fɔ gris in an mek i go mek am kwik
na nays man, i go mek am fayn fɔ yu
Mi mami, na so mi kin du o,
na di sistɛm

Na di sistɛm dis o, ɛn yu gɛt fɔ smat fɔ bit am
na fɔ kɔba yu ed mek yu fut sɛf go kɔba
Misɛf, we a nɔ kin go wok
a kin gi mi bɔs small tin fɔ mak mi nem
dɛn we mɔnt dɔn, a gi am in yon pasul
bo, na wi ɔl de na di sem pati;
na di sistɛm

Iii, bo dis bɔy gɛt dray yay o
i jis kam kɔt di layn
Somnan gɛt bad trik bo
i nɔ no si se wi ɔl ɔri
Lɛf am ya, aw fɔ du?
wi ɔl go rich
ɛn di ledi we de na di dɛsk tu slo
i jis de tok na in fon, i nɔ wan kno natin
ɛn luk am de tek sɛlfi sɛf
a kens sɛf.....
bɔt aw fɔ du, na di sistɛm.

THE END

98

www.ingramcontent.com/pod-product-compliance
Lightning Source LLC
Chambersburg PA
CBHW032143040426
42449CB00005B/387